CHOOSING A WEB HOST

How To Choose The Web Hosting Service That Is Best For You

Peter Laws

Choosing a Web Host

How to Choose the Web Hosting Service that is Best for You

by

Peter Laws

and

Gordon Goodfellow

Published by Inteltab Media

Email: admin@inteltab.com

ISBN-13: 978-1729840801

LEGAL NOTICE and TERMS of USE AGREEMENT

THIS EBOOK GUIDE IS DESIGNED TO HELP PEOPLE DECIDE HOW TO CHOOSE THE BEST WEB HOSTING SERVICE WHICH IS RIGHT FOR THEM, AND BREAKS THIS DOWN INTO THE VARIOUS ASPECTS OF WEB HOSTING WHICH SHOULD BE CONSIDERED WHEN CHOOSING SUCH A HOST.

POLICY OF CONSPICUOUS DISCLOSURE: WE RECEIVE COMPENSATION FROM THE COMPANIES WHOSE SERVICES WE REVIEW AND/OR DEMONSTRATE. WE TESTED THE WEB HOSTING SITE(S) MENTIONED HERE. WE ARE INDEPENDENTLY OWNED AND THE OPINIONS EXPRESSED HERE ARE OUR OWN.

NOTHING WITHIN THIS GUIDE IS INTENDED TO EXPRESS OR SIGNIFY ANY PROMISE OF EARNINGS, IMPLIED OR OTHERWISE. ALL INFORMATION IS SUPPLIED FOR EDUCATIONAL PURPOSES. IF YOU ARE USING A WEBSITE OR BLOGGING PLATFORM FOR BUSINESS PURPOSES THEN YOU SHOULD USE DUE DILIGENCE WHEN MAKING BUSINESS DECISIONS AND ALSO SEEK THE HELP OF A QUALIFIED AND INSURED PROFESSIONAL SUCH AS A LAWYER OR ACCOUNTANT OR OTHER BUSINESS ADVISER. NO GUARANTEES ARE MADE THAT YOU WILL ACHIEVE BUSINESS OR FINANCIAL SUCCESS BY SIMPLY BUILDING A WEBSITE, AND IT IS GENERALLY ACCEPTED THAT THE SUCCESS OF ANY VENTURE IS IN DIRECT PROPORTION TO THE AMOUNT OF EFFORT PUT INTO IT, SPECIAL EXPERIENCE AND KNOWLEDGE AND OTHER DECISIVE FACTORS.

THE AUTHOR AND PUBLISHER SHALL IN NO EVENT BE HELD LIABLE, AT ANY TIME, TO ANY PARTY, FOR ANY DIRECT, INDIRECT, PUNITIVE, SPECIAL, INCIDENTAL OR OTHER CONSEQUENTIAL DAMAGES ARISING DIRECTLY OR INDIRECTLY FROM ANY USE OF THIS MATERIAL, WHICH IS PROVIDED FOR EDUCATION USE ONLY AND ON AN 'AS IS' BASIS, AND WITHOUT ANY WARRANTIES WHATSOEVER.

NO PART OF THIS MAY BE COPIED, CHANGED IN ANY FORMAT, SOLD OR USED IN ANY WAY WITHOUT THE WRITTEN CONSENT OF THE AUTHOR.

Affiliate Disclosure and Transparency: Products and services recommended here may provide affiliate commission to the author. Affiliate commissions are always built into the pricing of a product or service, which means that not buying through an affiliate link does not mean that it can be bought cheaper! Almost all hosting companies have affiliate programs, therefore the field is level in any event: recommendations in this ebook are always made on merit, not on the fact that commission is payable to the author. Nevertheless, the author will receive a commission for recommending services in this book. But those recommendations will have been made anyway, as it is the same hosting service the author has decided to use himself, and he is very happy with it!

Contents

CHOOSING A WEB HOST 2

LEGAL NOTICE AND TERMS OF USE AGREEMENT 3

CONTENTS 5

INTRODUCTION 1

REASONS FOR CHOOSING A WEB HOST 2

RELIABILITY/DOWNTIME 4

DATA TRANSFER (TRAFFIC/BANDWIDTH) AND DISK SPACE 5

TECHNICAL SUPPORT 7

CONTROL PANEL (CPANEL) 9

FANTASTICO, FANTASTICO DELUXE AND SOFTACULOUS 11

SSL (SECURE SERVER), SHOPPING CART 15

EMAIL, AUTORESPONDERS, POP3, MAIL FORWARDING 16

MULTIPLE DOMAIN HOSTING AND SUBDOMAINS 18

SEO AND INTERNET MARKETING TOOLS 20

WEB HOSTING REVIEWS 22

COST: VALUE FOR MONEY 25

THE WEBSITE HOSTING SERVICE I RECOMMEND 26

FIRSTLY YOU NEED TO HAVE A DOMAIN NAME 28

OPENING YOUR ACCOUNT WITH INMOTION HOSTING 29

CONCLUSION 37

APPENDIX 38

Gordon Goodfellow is a writer, researcher, SEO, webmaster and affiliate practitioner. He has designed and built over 300 websites, and written several books and apps. He lives and works in London, U.K.

Peter Laws is his pen name.

Email: admin@inteltab.com

Introduction

Welcome to this short guide to help you choose the web hosting service which is the best for your needs.

Selecting the host which is right for your needs is a very important decision. Sometimes it has been described as the nearest thing to a marriage. The relationship you have with your web host, and the ability of your web host to deliver what you want it to deliver, is paramount in the way that your website or websites operate. You need your host to be responsive and fast in resolving issues. (In a perfect world you don't need those issues to appear in the first place.) You want to know that your host has the capability to handle other things down the line which you may not have heard of yet.

There's quite a lot of information in this guide, so my suggestion is to read all of it right through first of all. Then go back to the start and go through each section, implementing my recommendations as you do so. By reading this ebook online you will be able to access the resources I mention directly from your computer.

Sincerely wishing you the best,

Peter Laws

Reasons for Choosing a Web Host

When choosing a web host there are several things you must take into consideration. Some are more important than others; some may be of more importance to you because of the particular nature of what you have as a product or service (or even if you're just enthusiastic about something). Nevertheless, all aspects of the variety of things a web host has to offer should be considered. There may even be some things that you may not have thought about but which you may soon regard as essential a few months down the line.

You should compare hosts for each of the following aspects of their service.

If you lack any of the following then the effect could be detrimental to the functioning or appearance of your site or blog and the way in which your visitors may interact with it. If you have competitors then you will not want their hosts to provide them with the advantages and all the bells and whistles that you don't have. So it's very important to note that all the following aspects of hosting are important, irrespective of the type of website you have, or wish to have.

Broadly, these are:

Reliability/Downtime and speed of access
Data Transfer (Traffic/Bandwidth)

Technical support

Control Panel (cPanel)

Fantastico and Fantastico Deluxe (or equivalent such as Softaculous)

SSL (secure server), Shopping Cart

Email, Autoresponders, POP3, Mail Forwarding

Multiple Domain Hosting and Subdomains

SEO and Internet Marketing Tools

Web Hosting Reviews

Cost vs Value for Money

So let's consider these various aspects one by one.

Reliability/Downtime

First and foremost, this is one aspect which is completely non-negotiable! You need your website to be up and visible to anyone who wants to see it. This means that the site's 'downtime' needs to be as low as possible. Your site should load fast as well (there are a few things you can do to enhance load speed, such as have images which are not too large, pages which are not too long, etc., but the most important feature is the access time provided by your hosting service.

You should bear in mind that 99% uptime is too low; 99% sounds good at first, but it means that your website will be down for nearly four days a year. Is that acceptable to you? No, I didn't think so. It really should be 99.5% or better. Your host should be confident enough about this to guarantee a certain standard. In general, 99.9% uptime is acceptable to good. In reality, hosts who are confident enough to advertise 99.9% uptime are probably a lot better than that, if they are a well-known and reputable host.

Data Transfer (Traffic/Bandwidth) and Disk Space

Data transfer (sometimes known as "traffic" or "bandwidth") is the amount of information transferred from your site to visitors when they browse your site. This goes hand in hand with speed of access, so is really part of the same user-friendliness aspect of the hosting service. Certain types of website us up more bandwidth that others. For example, sites which have a lot of graphics on them use up a lot of space and bandwidth because of the size of graphics files, which are much larger than pages containing only text.

Most websites actually use less than 7 or 8 GBytes of bandwidth per month. Remember that your traffic requirements will probably grow over time. You want all those visitors, after all. So you don't want to keep having to check your bandwidth usage every other day. By hosting with a reputable company from the start you will find that you don't have to keep looking at this all on a regular basis.

Even though most websites will use only a few MBs of disk space, remember that you may want to put several sites on the same account at some later stage. You may also want, at a later stage, to expand some sites – perhaps adding subdomains to them, or plugging in things like forums and blogs onto the site, and all these take up space. Similar to the 'unlimited bandwidth' issue (see above) the unlimited disk space claims made by some hosting companies are not what they may seem to be. Again, check the small print. Establish exactly how much space is allocated per account. See if your hosting company offers differing sizes of space with differently priced accounts.

Technical support

For most people this is the most important consideration. Having a well-trained and responsive technical support team is essential. They must be fast to respond to your initial query, whatever it is, and they must also be quick in fixing whatever it is that has gone wrong, if such an error exists.

My own experience of host technical support has been very varied; from the excellent to the almost non-existent! In general, technical help is one of the things that make an impression on consumers more than anything else. It's almost as if the support personnel are ambassadors for that company; they are representatives in a real sense; they are your closest point of contact with that company. For this reason, a hosting service which has an inadequate support response is seen as slovenly and poor. They just couldn't be bothered. I can't believe that hosting companies don't realize this, and pay so little attention to their support system. The best technical support (by far) I've ever experienced with a budget hosting service is from InMotion. They are far and away the keenest, fastest and most knowledgeable. They're in a completely different league to some of the nightmare techie support staff of some other hosts (again, who shall be nameless) who seemed to be making it up as they went along!

So there are certain questions you need to ask of your hosting service. Does their technical support operate 24 hours a day, 7 days a week all year round? (This includes weekends and public holidays.) If they offer less than this, then stay away and choose another service.

Control Panel (cPanel)

Any hosting service worth its salt will have a control panel. I've noticed that the best and most organized hosts have a control panel standard known as cPanel as a regular feature within its user account. This is because everything seems to be included here in the same location: cPanel is a user-friendly interface which allows hosting customers to have access to all sorts of facilities and services within their account. Its scope is huge. These are some of the facilities available from cPanel:

Support center: live chat, tech support, billing, web templates, ticketing system;
Preferences: change the look and feel of your interface;
Mail: email addresses, mail forwarders, spam filtering, autoresponders, mailing lists, webmail;
File Manager (including backups, disk space manager and FTP accounts);
Logs: check bandwidth and your visitor numbers, integration with Webalizer and Awstats;
Domain Manager: addon domains, sub domains and domain redirects;
Security: password manager, IP blocking and various security necessities;
Databases (MySQL databases for serious data handling and other applications);
SEO and Marketing tools;
Frontpage extensions, cron jobs (for timed events) and PHP;
Perl, Ruby on Rails, Sitebuilder, error pages;
Fantastico/Fantastico Deluxe.

So if your host comes with cPanel then they will also automatically come with all the above features, and possible more.

Fantastico, Fantastico Deluxe and Softaculous

In particular, Fantastico (or Fantastico Deluxe) is a must-have facility within cPanel which allows you to set up and install software applications on your site with just a few clicks of your mouse. There are equivalents of Fantastico, such as Softaculous and QuickInstall, which do much the same thing.

Basically, this facility allows you to quickly and easily set up applications which are integrated into your account without the additional and fiddly work normally needed, such as manually setting up MySQL databases, configuring accounts, etc. Because Fantastico (or equivalent) is integrated as part of your specific account it knows exactly what to do in terms of integration and configuration and so works as a 'smart' tool requiring only a few clicks of the mouse and a few typed instructions from the user.

With Fantastico or Softaculous you can easily set up the following facilities (these are the ones currently offered in my cPanel Softaculous on my InMotion account):

Blogs (a choice of over 16 blog brands including the excellent *WordPress*);

Forums including the popular phpBB and a dozen other types;

Content Management (including Drupal, Geeklog, Joomla, Mambo, PHP-Nuke, PHP-Fusion, phpWCMS, phpWebSite, Siteframe, TYPO3, Xoops and over 50 others);

Customer Support (various helpdesks and ticketing systems including a choice of Help Center Live, osTicket, PerlDesk and Malan Support);

E-Commerce (Your own shopping cart. You can use Magento, CubeCart, OpenCart, SimpleInvoices, osCommerce or Zen Cart among many others);

Image Galleries (An Image Gallery system featuring categories and albums, thumbnails and intermediate size pictures, search features, new and random pictures, user management user comments, e-cards feature, slideshow viewer.

Mailing Lists: PHPlist is pre-installed.

Wiki (install your own wiki on your site with TikiWiki CMS/Groupware or PhpWiki)

Guest Books with eight types to choose from;

Other Scripts available which are all pre-installed in InMotion's version of Fantastico Deluxe include Dew-NewPHPLinks, Moodle, Open-Realty, OpenX, phpFormGenerator and WebCalendar. Project Management, Video, Educational, Gaming, Ad management and social networking applications are also there.

Some of the above software and other terms may be unfamiliar to you at the moment. But problems start when you learn that you need something and then you find that your host doesn't provide it! I've experienced this when I was a newbie several years ago and on several occasions.

Once was when I tried to install a blog on a site, and found that it didn't work. After lots of emails to the useless support center I was told that it was because I didn't have PHP 5. I didn't know what PHP 5 was. When I asked my (then) host I was told that they had PHP 4 but not PHP 5. In that case, I told them, why don't you upgrade to PHP 5? After a few days they wrote back to me and said that it wasn't their policy to run PHP 5, and that they would remain with PHP 4.

I switched my hosting company then and there to a better one. You don't have to be an expert to know when your hosting company is rubbish; you just have to have that feeling of knowing you've lost out.

But how do you know that you may need these things at some point in the future? Well, you don't. But I have a policy of making sure that my hosting service has the potential for upgrading. That's the only way that I know I won't have to waste time switching hosts in the future. Just **go for the host which has the best potential**, including the best customer support, but which still has a budget hosting plan which is very affordable.

SSL (secure server), Shopping Cart

SSL stands for secure socket layer or secure server. If you plan on doing any sort of business through your site, you must make sure your host has this facility as you will certainly need this if you plan to accept credit cards on your site. Check that the hosting service (and the package or plan that you intend to sign up for) has this as an option. Sometimes it is available as an extra to your hosting plan, and sometimes it is included as part of the package. For example, the InMotion Business package includes SSL and free SSL certificates, as it is expected that a business plan will be for business purposes including ecommerce!

Having an SSL certificate is a must-have these days, as it gives your website the coveted https:// at the start of its domain name. Search engines such as Google have also made it clear that they will give SSL sites better rankings, so you'll get a better listing in the search results – meaning more web visitors and more revenue – if your site has SSL.

Email, Autoresponders, POP3, Mail Forwarding

You should ensure that your host offers you at least 50 email addresses with each site that you host with the, though more is better. For example, you might want a separate email address for admin@yoursite.com, enquiries@yoursite.com, sales@yoursite.com, technical@yoursite.com, accounts@yoursite.com, support@yoursite.com as well as several others. Even if there is just one person running the site, it's useful to separate these functions to know what each incoming email is about and to compartmentalize any tasks.

If you have other people working on or associated with the website you would be advised to have more than 50 email addresses, so that you can give each person their own email address within the organization, for example bob.marketing@yoursite.com and so on. The better hosts usually have provision for up to 100 or more email addresses per domain (site).

You will also want to be able to redirect these email addresses to a main address, if you need to do that. This will be much easier to look after centrally than having to access different mailboxes all the time. Emails may be sent to one central address as well as to individual inboxes if required. Your host should be able to do all of this with no problem.

Does your host offer autoresponders? This is where anyone sending an email to you will automatically receive a pre-written email back thanking them or acknowledging their enquiry. This is not only courteous but professional, of course. It shows that you care about looking after people who enquire about your website, whether they are existing client, prospective clients or not.

You should be able to redirect your domain-based emails to your regular email software client (such as Outlook, etc.) without any difficulty. You should also be able to add passwords to each email account, for extra security. You should be able to add, delete and manage all your email accounts from a central location, including changing your passwords in a secure manner whenever you wish to do so. All this needs to be simple; you don't want to have to contact Support every time you need to change a password. Such things should be intuitively laid out in a user-friendly manner on your control panel.

Incidentally, all of the above are available in the Mail section of InMotion's cPanel.

Multiple Domain Hosting and Subdomains

It is quite possible to host more than one website per hosting account as long as that account is equipped to do so. Most hosting services worth their salt will have enough disk space and other facilities for accounts with provision for many sites (domains) and some for unlimited domains.

A subdomain is a domain resting within an existing domain. It takes the form www.subdomain.mainsite.com with a period separating the subdomain element from the main domain name. This is very useful if you want to have various subjects or sectors of interest within your website without having to register extra domains all the time. Subdomains used in this way are free (no need to pay to register them with a domain registration service) and the SEO advantages of having subdomains as opposed to inner pages on your existing site is that each subdomain is given equal weight and importance by the search engines, while the original domain maintains its own authority.

So, if you were to have an insurance site, you may want to have subdomains for the various types of insurance you have an interest in. For example:

www.buildingsinsurance.goodinsurancequotes.com
www.carinsurance.goodinsurancequotes.com
www.healthinsurance.goodinsurancequotes.com

www.holidayinsurance.goodinsurancequotes.com

Each of the subdomains requires no extra domain costs as it is 'piggy backing' on your main domain name. The other advantage of subdomains is that you don't have to worry about whether the domain name will be available for you to register; if it is tacked onto the front of your existing domain then it will **always** be available for you to use exclusively, whatever it is.

Another useful application of subdomains is where your website supplies can be described by several search terms and you can't decide which one to use for your domain name. With subdomains you can use all of them!

For example:

www.heatingengineer.engineeringservices-yourtown.com
www.centralheatinginstallation.engineeringservices-yourtown.com
www.centralheatingsystems.engineeringservices-yourtown.com
www.heatingexpert.engineeringservices-yourtown.com
www.homeheating.engineeringservices-yourtown.com

Your hosting company should be able to allow you to add subdomains to any of your existing domains quickly and easily through your control panel. Hosts which use cPanel have this all within the Domains section.

SEO and Internet Marketing Tools

SEO stands for search engine optimization (or optimization) and is the part-art and part-science which allows websites to get high positions or rankings within the search engines within the search engine results pages (SERPS). SEO is not difficult, although it has acquired the status of being a bit of a dark art.

On-page optimization involves getting the right elements onto your web pages so that the search engines know what you site or blog is about and emphasizing these elements so that they achieve prominence. It also requires a good internal linking structure and solid site architecture. Off-page optimization is basically getting links from other websites and blogs which all contribute to give your own website the authority needed for good rankings. SEO is a huge subject, so I won't even attempt to get more specific than this, except to say that both on-page and off-page SEO are vital if your website or blog is to be a success.

Most good hosting companies will go that little bit further and offer their customers SEO and Internet marketing (IM) tools of various sorts. This may vary from company to company, but will usually include some form of Google sitemap tool which can quickly be used to make a sitemap for your website(s) which you can then submit to Google to ensure that all the pages on your site(s) are indexed by that search engine.

Such tools also may include search engine submission services, directory submission services and data site (Alexa.com etc.) submission services. These are also useful for getting valid links back to your website and increasing the site visibility in the search engines. It should be noted that, of late, such submission processes do not count for much in terms of SEO, although they certainly help with speed of indexing.

Most web hosts will allow you to see the major basic metrics of your website or blog. For hosts which use cPanel there is a section which gives you raw access logs which are needed for using certain third-party software applications which tell you about visitor behaviour, etc. Used in conjunction with marketing tools, notably Google Analytics, these are powerful utilities to help you both get more visitors to your website and also to achieve a better conversion rate with whatever targets you have set.

Web Hosting Reviews

It is always worth the effort of checking out what others have to say about each web hosting service which catches your eye. There are forums dedicated to hosting where you can follow user's real-life experiences of good and bad hosts and learn from these. There are also many newsgroups where you can enjoy similar experiences from first-hand knowledge. The thing about hosting is that it is so crucial to a website's performance that it gets under people's skin. All good experiences are praised and all bad experiences are damned. There is little room for grey areas on forums: opinion tends to be polarized and either a host is good or bad.

Standard reviews are also useful as well, but there is nothing like an impassioned thread in a forum to enjoy vicariously the real-life experiences of someone who has been let down or pleasantly surprised by what their host has done. Learn from all of these. Put yourself in these users' shoes. From what they've learned you can learn too, except it isn't going to cost you the money that they've already paid out to learn it!

One immediate advantage of going to the forums and newsgroups is that you will quickly learn which hosts to **avoid**. This is because there will be so many complaints about them. Usually these hosts will fall down in one or two areas, and these will be the areas that people will be complaining about most. The name of that host will come up again and again if it is associated with a particular problem or shortcoming.

You can subscribe to threads on most forums and newsgroups, so that you are sent an email automatically whenever there is a new posting or someone has added to the debate.

You might also have a look at a site called Quora and also Yahoo Answers. Type in the name of the web host you want to find out about in the search box. You're bound to get some silly answers, but among the chaff there will be some nuggets of wisdom. The chances are, if a host is recommended for customer service, technical support, software support, bandwidth, costing structure and bandwidth, then the chances are that this host is a pretty good one to follow up.

There are only a handful of hosting services that people are so happy with that they write about them in forums and newsgroups. There are even fewer hosts which people are actually passionate about. You can feel this passion in how they write about them. These are the hosts to really look out for, because these are the hosts which over-deliver and the ones you know you can trust all the time.

You should also note that hosts can be very popular for years and then suddenly they lose their status. This may be due to being taken over by a larger company. Without naming names, there is one host in particular who used to be great but now is sadly quite mediocre. There's nothing to be done about those, unfortunately; the new corporate owner will trim the best off the service to gain more profits and the quality of service will always suffer.

Cost: Value for Money

The old adage, "you get what you pay for" is highly relevant when it comes to web hosting. But it is also true that some hosts give you better value for money than others. Many people will find themselves drawn to the host with the best customer support or technical support; and it's not necessarily true that the costliest hosts are the best.

Certainly you will want to make sure that any host you consider has all the above attributes, and room for more: because there's no point in paying even a minimum amount per month and getting a hosting service which doesn't totally work to your satisfaction. Customer and technical support is also an important consideration; otherwise what are you paying for?

Unless you want a dedicated server for your website (which is not at all necessary in most cases) we'll be looking at budget plans that are within most pockets. The good news is that you **will** be able to get a hosting package for **less than $6 a month** which offers everything you could possibly want, with unlimited domains (websites), unlimited bandwidth, cPanel with Fantastico/Softaculous as well as superb customer service which will treat you as if you were the only customer in the world. More of them later.

The Website Hosting Service I Recommend

Having read this far, it probably won't come as a surprise to you that I recommend InMotion hosting. Having used the Internet since the final years of the last century, I have used many hosting services. It is true to say that the standards in the hosting industry in general have improved steadily, always due to rising competition; better services have tended to beat older services who do not come up to scratch with their customers, and this has been the rising trend since the beginning of the Internet.

Indeed, even around the early years of this century there were still charlatans who purposely misled their customers about what was on offer, and infamously presented them with costly and unexpected bills, usually for bandwidth usage in excess of what was provided as 'normal'. These companies fell by the wayside as word got around about their unfair practices. Happily, over time, these bandits have left the scene.

There are other services which were highly regarded for years but which, for one reason and another (a major reason being corporate takeovers) fell by the wayside as their standards dropped. I'm not naming names here but people who have been around for a few years will know who I'm talking about. But let's forget about these also-rans; they are now in the past.

InMotion was started in 2001 and is owned and run by their employees. It is a U.S. company, a 3-star CNET service provider and member of the Better Business Bureau. InMotion has won many awards in the industry and their team is headed and manned by technology experts, not bean counters. Their technical support staff go through vigorous training and are comprehensively qualified in all relevant fields. It goes without saying that they are all U.S. based and that their native language is English!

Discovering InMotion, after my experience of other services previously considered 'very good', was wonderfully refreshing, and I can honestly recommend them to anyone who is serious about their business. If you don't have prior knowledge of hosting then you probably won't notice how good they are; but if you have had a working knowledge of the hosting business then I hope that you will feel the same way as I did soon after you open an account and speak to them.

I should also add that all the good hosting companies worth their salt have affiliate program, and people like me who review hosting services are members of their affiliate programs. This means that when people buy services which I recommend I get paid a commission for the sale. If you buy a hosting package from InMotion through my links then I get a commission and thereby I can pay my bills. I need to mention this because of FTC rules about recommending goods and services. But, then again, I use this hosting company myself for my own websites. So I even recommend InMotion to me! I like them because of the reasons given, and I'd be recommending them irrespective of their affiliate program. I just needed to say that.

Firstly You Need to Have a Domain Name

You should choose a domain name which is as close as possible to the search phrase that you wish to be found for on the search engines. It should be a search term that someone would use if they were on the Internet and trying to find the product or service that you offered. You may want to pick a domain which incorporates your city if you offer a local service (i.e. 'Tax Advisor Cambridge' or 'Landscape Gardening Boston').

Before you open any hosting account you will need to register a domain name. InMotion say that they can *"can register any .com, .net, .org, .us, .biz, or .info domain and can support any domain on the net."* You can register any one of these for FREE when you open your hosting account. You cannot register UK domains for free, however. So if you wanted a .uk, .co.uk, .org.uk, .me.uk, .net.uk, .ltd.uk or .plc.uk domain name you would need to register this elsewhere (such as 123-Reg) and then host it on your InMotion account. At the time of writing 123-Reg were offering .co.uk domains at £0.99 for the first year.

You may find that your domain name is not available because it has been registered by someone else. If that is the case then pick another variant of the search term. You can always use hyphens between words if you wish.

Opening Your Account with InMotion Hosting

Click here to go to InMotion. You'll see a screen like the one below. (If you are reading this as a hard copy, go to the end of this book for my affiliate link if you think that my work here has been useful to you and you want to reward me with an honest day's pay!)

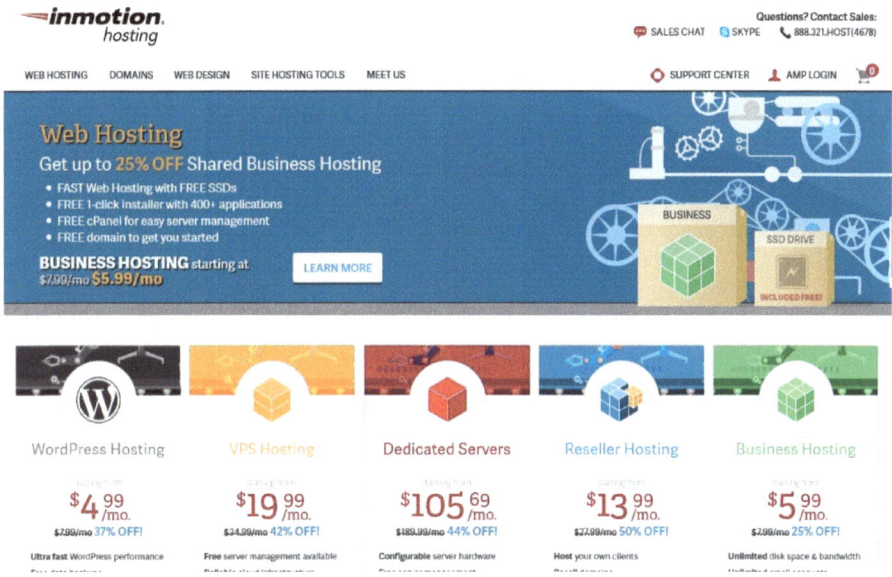

InMotion has several hosting packages available. These are Wordpress Hosting, VPS Hosting, Dedicated Servers, Reseller Hosting and Business Hosting. Here we're concerned with their Business Hosting package. So click on the Business Hosting package on the right and you'll see the following screen:

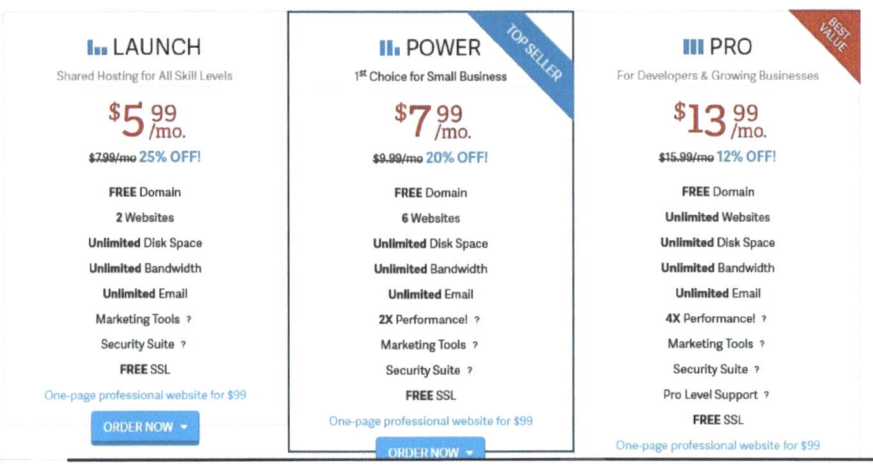

Here you can see that the Launch package will allow you two websites in the same hosting account, and gives you unlimited disk space and unlimited bandwidth, with unlimited email. It also includes a free SSL (the coveted https:// prefix to your site) which means it is a secure site. The Power package gives you room for six websites and is slightly more expensive and twice as fast, but the Launch package is perfectly adequate at this stage. You can always upgrade later if you wish. The standards that InMotion set are very high, so if they say that something is adequate they mean much more than just adequate!

So, Launch, Power or Pro: it's entirely up to you to decide.

Now if you hover your mouse over the version you wish to order you'll see that the price stated is slightly different if you pay for one year's service rather than two. It works out cheaper per month if you pay for two years up front. (At different times this varies: you may find a special offer exists at the time of your purchase.)

Next you'll be taken to the secure checkout. Here you *may* be presented with an upsell offer (depending on whether such an offer is running at the time). This will be to upgrade at very little cost. This is why I recommend clicking on the lowest costing option – because you may well get the offer which allows you to upgrade to the more powerful version at a very light increase in price. For the kind of upgrade in power and versatility you experience this will be well worth it!

Anyway, it's up to you whether you upgrade or not, obviously. Next you will see a screen which allows you to configure your server. If you have no particular preference here just leave it at the default settings.

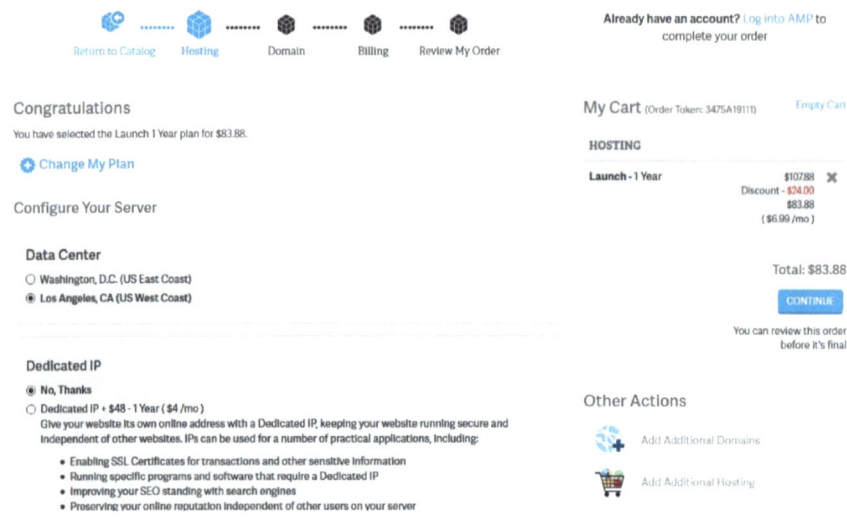

When you click the Continue button you will be presented with the screen which asks you to either enter the domain name that you already have or indicate that you would like to purchase a new domain (see below). Assuming that your research into getting the best domain name has been completed, you should select the lower radio button and enter your chosen domain name into the box. Then click on the Continue button to go to the next screen which asks you if you are

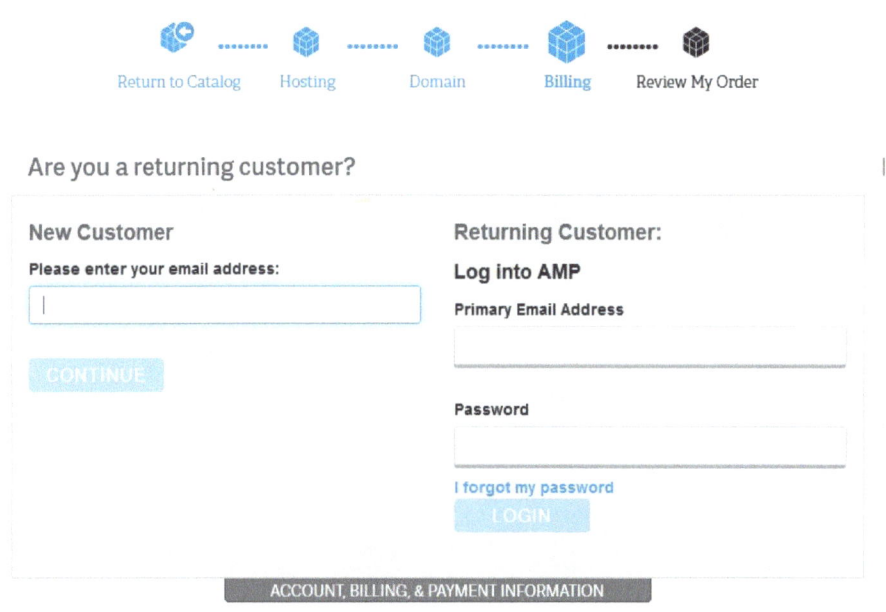

a new customer or a returning customer. Assuming that you are a new customer you should enter your email address in the New Customer field and click Continue to go to the Account, Billing and Payment section. Fill in your contact details (below) and then scroll down to the payment section to complete the process.

You now have a brand-new InMotion hosting account with your domain name all set to go!

There are a couple of things you need to do at your registrar's site before your website becomes live. Depending on what type of domain extension you have (you may have opted to get a free .com name from InMotion or you may have registered a .co.uk or some other extension at another domain registrar) you might have to unlock the domain if it is a .com in cases where the domain in being transferred. But don't worry; your registrar will have full documentation on how to complete the full process, and possibly a video showing you in real-time how it is done.

Account, Billing & Payment Information

Complete your account information

First Name:

Last Name:

Company Name:
(*Optional*)

Country: Select Your Country

Address Line 1:

Address Line 2:
(*Optional*)

City:

Phone:
(ex. 222-555-1212 for USA)

Email: inteltab@btinternet.com

Confirm Email:

Referred By:
(*Optional*)

While still at the registrar site you will now need to point the nameservers to your hosting service's nameservers. This will involve entering the names of two nameservers into two different fields. If there are any other matters to be taken care of, or if you are unsure about anything at this stage (which hasn't already been covered here) then you can send an email to InMotion to ask them or look up InMotion's FAQs. Better still, you'll probably prefer to get the whole thing over with as quickly as possible, which is where InMotion's excellent online chat facility comes in very useful. (And here you'll see just what a quality hosting service this is: it's always in the online live support that the quality of a hosting service is best seen.

The InMotion nameservers will resemble the following:

> ns1.inmotionhosting.com
> ns2.inmotionhosting.com

The setup of your domain and hosting is now complete. Leave it a short while - a couple of hours to be safe, though it should be quicker than that - and your site's details will have propagated through the entire Internet. Now whatever you upload to your site's server will be visible, as your website, anywhere on the Internet.

Conclusion

I hope you've enjoyed reading this short guide to choosing a web hosting service. Hopefully by now you will be in a much better position to match one host against another, and have opened an account with the hosting service which is best for your business and its growing needs.

I have weighted the debate heavily towards InMotion in these pages, as my own experience dictates that this is the best host for most purposes. They certainly offer everything I've ever needed in my 18 + years of hosting websites and blogs. As I mentioned before, InMotion pay me through their affiliate program to recommend their service, but so do all the other quality hosting companies, and I'm recommending InMotion because I think that they are the best over all the others. I can only hope that you have just as fine an experience of them as I've done over the years.

Sincerely wishing you the best in all your endeavours,

Peter Laws

Appendix

Here is my affiliate link for logging into InMotion and setting up your own hosting account there.

http://bit.ly/inmotiongsg

Thanks!

www.ingramcontent.com/pod-product-compliance
Lightning Source LLC
Chambersburg PA
CBHW040249220526
45473CB00001B/421